snapshot·picture·library

TRUCKS

snapshot·picture·library

TRUCKS

FOG CITY PRESS

Published by Fog City Press,
a division of Weldon Owen Inc.
415 Jackson Street
San Francisco, CA 94111 USA
www.weldonowen.com

WELDON OWEN INC.
Group Publisher, Bonnier Publishing Group John Owen
President, CEO Terry Newell
Senior VP, International Sales Stuart Laurence
VP, Sales and New Business Development Amy Kaneko
VP, Publisher Roger Shaw
VP, Creative Director Gaye Allen
Executive Editor Elizabeth Dougherty
Assistant Editor Sarah Gurman
Senior Designer William Mack
Production Director Chris Hemesath
Production Manager Michelle Duggan
Color Manager Teri Bell

A WELDON OWEN PRODUCTION
© 2008 Weldon Owen Inc.

Library of Congress Control Number: 2008935242

ISBN: 978 1-74089-856-0

10 9 8 7 6 5 4 3 2
2009 2010 2011 2012

Printed by Tien Wah Press in Singapore.

Day or night, trucks never stop working. Trucks carry all the things we need in our daily lives.

Trucks take our food from farmers and factories to supermarkets. They plow snow in winter, work on construction sites, and help build houses. They clear away garbage to keep our world clean.

You can see trucks being busy all around the land. Do you have a favorite kind of truck?

Trucks come in all
kinds of shapes,
sizes, and colors.
Each one is made
to do its own
very special job.

Most trucks are big, but some are really big. "Big rigs" have lots of wheels.

The front part
of a truck is
called a tractor.
The tractor
pulls the trailer
along behind.

Trucks are built to travel long distances, from sunny deserts to snowy mountains.

The driver
sits in the cab.
Drivers can
stop and rest
in a little room
at the back if
they get tired.

The cab has lights, horns, and shiny exhaust pipes. Without its trailer, the tractor looks very bare.

Trailers are loaded using a forklift. Sometimes the forklift drives straight up the ramp.

Some trailers
are loaded with
goods straight
from a factory
or warehouse.

Have you seen trucks on busy highways? When you see an empty truck you know it's on the way to get a new load.

This big truck is called a tank truck. Its long trailer is shaped like a tube. It carries liquids like milk, oil, or gasoline.

Tanks come
in all sizes
and shapes.

This truck is at the docks. It is waiting to be loaded with goods that have come from another country on a ship.

The goods
are packed
in big metal
containers,
which are put
on the back
of the truck.

Road trains haul lots of trailers at once. They are common on the long empty roads in Australia.

This road train is crossing the desert. The journey is a long one, and the tractor is pulling two big trailers behind it.

A pickup or a small cargo truck is handy for carrying a small load or just cruising around town.

Tow trucks
rescue cars that
have broken
down and take
them away.

Car transporters
take new cars from
the factory where
they're made to the
car dealer where
they're sold.

Street sweepers clean our roads. Garbage trucks take away trash.

Dump trucks
carry soil, sand,
and gravel at
building sites.

These massive earth-moving trucks are used for mining.

These loggers are transporting trees. The wood will be turned into paper and new furniture.

The drums on cement-mixers turn to stop the concrete in them from getting hard!

Snowplows
work hard in
the winter,
clearing snow
from the roads.

Monster trucks play hard in the summer, performing at outdoor shows.

Monster trucks crush cars, jump in the air, and perform tricks!

While everyone's asleep, trucks drive on through the night.

Trailer

A trailer is the back part of a truck that holds cargo. A semi-trailer has wheels only at the rear end. A tractor supports the front end when they're attached.

Tractor

A tractor is the front part of the truck that pulls the trailer. A tractor pulling a trailer can be called a semi, a tractor-trailer, a big rig, or an 18-wheeler, for instance.

Tank truck

Tank trucks can refrigerate their load or keep it in a pressurized environment. They're the best kind of truck for carrying a large amount of a liquid like gasoline.

Road train

Some of the biggest trucks are road trains, which pull more than one trailer. They're commonly used in remote areas and are popular in Australia.

Pickup truck

Pickup trucks are small trucks with an open cargo area in back. Often a rear gate folds down to make loading easier. Some people drive a pickup instead of a car.

Garbage truck

Garbage trucks have a smelly job. They all collect trash, and some collect recycling, too. You can spot them driving around very early in the morning!

Dump truck

Construction workers use dump trucks a lot to move materials such as dirt, gravel, and sand. The back part is an open tray, which tilts to tip a load out.

Mining truck

The biggest dump trucks are mining trucks. They're huge! Digging machines and large excavators fill these giant trucks with large amounts of earth to haul away.

Logging truck

When trees are cut down, the logs are placed onto the back of logging trucks to be taken to a factory. Iron bars at the sides keep the logs from falling out.

Cement-mixer

Cement-mixers combine cement, sand or gravel, and water to make concrete. Their drums turn continually to keep the concrete from getting hard!

Snowplow

Snowplows clear snow off roads, parking lots, and even driveways. A truck's plow pushes snow out of the way, just like a bulldozer's blade moves dirt.

Monster truck

Monster trucks aren't for driving around town—their super-sized wheels can crush cars! Their drivers show off by racing and performing stunts at car rallies.

ACKNOWLEDGMENTS

Weldon Owen would like to thank the staff at Toucan Books Ltd, London, for their assistance in the production of this book: Ellen Dupont, managing director; Jo Bourne, author; Thomas Keenes, designer; and Hannah Bowen, project manager and researcher.

CREDITS